Muted Explanations

CONTENTS

OF
ACKNOWLEDGMENTS

Thank you
Karla
for loving and encouraging me through everything

Abby, Amelia, Owen, Levi
for being my favorite people and enduring a father
in perpetual training

My parents
for raising me in the nurture and admonition of the Lord

My wife Karla and our friend Lora
for kindly editing this book

The Youth I taught over the years
for growing with me & helping me learn to share Scripture
with emotion and context
(it took a while)

OF
INTRODUCTIONS

My wife, Karla, has been showing me pictures of these
ultra-cute, puffy sheep.
She believes that because the algorithm keeps showing her
more sheep, that means we need them.
I thought you should know that first.

Hello!
My name is Dwayne.
I hope this book finds you well.
I wrote it to start a dialogue with you:
one of emotion, Scripture, and context.

I recently "retired" from twenty years of full-time youth ministry.
It was rewarding, challenging, and developing.
The above "thought you should know" paragraph probably clued
you in that you are reading the thoughts of one who has spent a bit
of his life on the outskirts of the pastoral Venn diagram. One who
believes in the truth of Scripture and love of God, but maybe veers
far from both the 'sophisticated' and 'cool' circles. I wave an
enthusiastically reserved "Hi!" from the nerdy/creative sphere.

When it comes to conversations concerning emotion, Scripture, and
context, often folks like to talk about one or two of these subjects
without the other. It could be in personal conversations, in
teaching, preaching, small group discussions or the like. It may be
addressing Scripture as more of an intellectual inquiry, sometimes
including the context of the passage, other times not, using
"deep study" of a verse or two to focus on a particular topic.
But truth is found in the contextual melody.
The what's and why's behind the how's.
And Scripture is paved with emotion.
Feelings resound from the very stones of the Christian walk.
Sidelining them leads to forgetting in Whose image we are made.

So let us converse in lyrical verse.

That may lead to a Seussian lifestyle if taken beyond these pages, but for today, our dialogue will be melodic!

Lyrical verse has a way of pulling all three: emotion, Scripture, and context to the front of our minds. By all means, other ways of communicating do this too, but for me, lyrics have been the strongest way to share these three with others… and even myself.

I have taught from many an outline over the past twenty years, crafted many lessons, sermons, lectures, and workshops. Most were not poetic, but lyric has a way of focusing thought. Rhythm feeds progression. The limiting nature of meter and rhyme frees one to harness feelings and present purpose.

So, let's start a conversation. I'll present to you lyrics of feelings and Scripture focused on real emotion, based in the context of the Truth of Scripture and the life God has given us. I'll also share a few bonus lyrics from other parts of my brain; they will be shared with you from the land outside the Venn diagram. A place where many of us, and maybe you, dwell. Then you can continue the conversation, weaving emotion and context into your discussions of Scripture and life with others. I'm looking forward to hearing it as it makes its way around the edges of the Venn diagram and back around, and hopefully, it will make its emotional way through the logical middle as well.

As you read these lyrics, you may wonder if they were created with a certain musical meter in mind?

The answer is: yes.

I wrote each one with a melody, tune, and musical progression.

For some, I put that melody down and you can actually hear them if you'd like. (They're the ones with the * at the end of the title. You can find them under my name online.)

For the rest, feel free to make up your own or use the default melody in your head. You know, that music you use to fill in the gaps when your thinking. It could be a commercial jingle, a show tune, song or whatever. If your unsure, you're more than welcome to use my default melody, the theme to The Fresh Prince of Bel-Air.

Works for just about everything in a pinch.

Now let's talk some emotional, contextual Scripture… and fonts!

This is going to be fun.

OF
DOCTRINE &
UNDER
STANDING

In My Finite Understanding

Lord, You're more, than my mind can grasp,
But You made my mind, to understand, so finitely
And You, oh Lord, dwell outside of time,
But You made my life, to tick away, by hourly

My heart can sink,
when I start to think
that I will never truly fathom
Your boundlessness,
and I confess,
my knowledge feels so wildly random
But joy comes when I realize You created me to know…

That your grace is greater than my comprehending
Your provision breaks the scope of all my planning
And your awesomeness transcends the bounds
of sin & hope & mercy
And when I think I know enough,
I'll still be learning
In my finite understanding.

As I grow in grace and in the Word,
You show me more, of who You are, and what You do
The vastness of Your love fills me with joy
And humbles me, to look past myself and more at You

And You require,
that my desire,
involves the reading of Your Word
So my faith in You,
will be renewed,
and I will overcome the world
But that knowledge in itself is not the joy that I now know…

For your grace is greater than my comprehending
Your provision breaks the scope of all my planning
And your awesomeness transcends the bounds
of sin & hope & mercy
And when I think I know enough,
I'll still be learning
In my finite understanding.

It's like seeing the sun shining large in the sky
Knowing that if you left today
On a sun-bound drive, cruisin' at 65,
In a space-worthy car slash plane
On day two hundred seventy-seven,
you'd finally arrive
And just like math, your vastness blows my mind
And just like math, your vastness blows my mind

For your grace is greater than my comprehending
Your provision breaks the scope of all my planning
And your awesomeness transcends the bounds
of sin & hope & mercy
So I study in your Word
and I keep learning
In my finite understanding.

The power and wonder of omniscience.

To know all what is, was, and will be

The cause, effect, and observer.

Outlying the scope of humanity.

At all points, beyond comprehension
Being outside the fourth dimension
And You loved us still
Even when my faith shows frailty
At all points, beyond comprehension
Being outside the fourth dimension
And You wrote us in
Knowing all the trouble we would be

He is good, good in all time
He is good, good in all time
God You are good, in every point,
all along the line
You are good, good in all time.

The setting and rising of the sun
    Ushers in our host of memory
        But You are present in all those days this hour
            In resurrection, oh Your face I'll see.

At all points, beyond comprehension
Being outside the fourth dimension
And You loved us still
Even when my faith shows frailty
At all points, beyond comprehension
Being outside the fourth dimension
And You wrote us in
Knowing all the trouble we would be

He is good, good in all time
He is good, good in all time
God You are good, in every point,
        all along the line
You are good, good in all time.

Sons, Not Slaves
Romans 8:12-17

I am
Sinking
down as
a slave

My value
dispersed
my family
erased

My fearful
Existence
so simply
replaced

I am
bound
I'm brought
down

Sin O
that master
that holds me
in chains

Bound to
that tyrant
for all of
my days

Worked 'til
I'm useless
then tossed in
the grave

I am
bound
I'm brought
down

Purchased
redemption
adopted
as son

Given
this honor
by nothing
I've done

Justified
fully
through Jesus
the Son

I am
found
I am
found

Owned
my rights given to another
Sold
only worth what I can offer
Serve
without care or consent
When I can't produce
I become worthless
Scared

but then my chains were broken

Free

by the power of adoption

Live

as an heir of the Father

witness Spirit born

we belong to no other

We cry out, "Abba, Father!"
We cry out, "Abba, Father!"
For we're the heirs of God
We cry out, "Abba, Father!"

Jesus, Who Are You?
John 7; Matthew 11:28-12:14

Jesus, who are you?
Who are you?
Who are you?
Some say,
A good man is he
Others amazed
that he hadn't studied
Jesus, who are you?
Who are you?
Who are you?
Will Christ do more signs
than this man today?
Or is he leading
the people astray?
Jesus, who are you?
Who are you?
Who are you?
Are you greater
than father Abraham?
Did you just claim
that you are I Am?
Jesus, who are you?

Who are you?

Who are you?

Who are you?

Now the time had come,
for the Feast of the Jews
A time to remember,
by sitting in booths
And the leaders of faith,
had fallen to pride
Viewed Jesus a threat,
and called for his life
But the crowds weren't sure,
in whom to believe
Surprised by the fact,
he was able to speak
As they knew of the threat,
yet he spoke openly
We know where he's from,
but who could he be?

The crowd there was troubled,
as they knew that he
Had healed on the Sabbath,
Law breaking it seemed
So Jesus answered
my teaching's not mine
It comes from the Father,
and it's not my time
And on the matter,
of a Sabbath's break
Cov'nant signs and healing,
both are good that day
To know the Father,
and know His true plan
I'm Lord of the Sabbath,
and Sabbath's for man.

Jesus, who are you?

So Much More Than Manna
John 6:1-71

I am the bread of life
Who ever eats this bread will
Never hunger again
I am the bread of life
This bread comes down from heaven
So much more than manna
So much more than manna

The day before, up on a mountain
On the other side of Galilee's Sea
A crowd gathered, following after
When they heard of the sick He was healing
The people, they were hungry
Jesus looked up and saw their need
Fed the whole crowd, a miracle of bread and fish
They cried, "The true Prophet indeed!"

After Jesus had done this...
The disciples, sailed back
Jesus walked upon the sea
The crowds weren't ready to hear
Him say...

I am the bread of life
Who ever eats this bread will
Never hunger again
I am the bread of life
This bread comes down from heaven
So much more than manna
So much more than manna

That next day, in Capernaum
Those on that side of the sea
Could not surmise how Jesus got there
And the mountain crowd came so they too could feed
They only came to see more wonders
Jesus told them to believe
They desired a sign of manna
Jesus said, "I give you me"

After Jesus told them this...
Many disciples, of Jesus
Turned back
And no longer followed Him
Cuz He said...

I am the bread of life
Who ever eats this bread will
Never hunger again
I am the bread of life
This bread comes down from heaven
So much more than manna
So much more than manna

Do you want eternal life?
Do you want to be raised on the last day?
You must eat my flesh,
you must drink my blood
An internal saving faith
Not the bread your fathers ate
They ate, they died,
That bread from heaven did not change their fate
I bring internal saving faith

So much more than manna
So much more than manna

No Respecter of Persons
(aka God Does Not)
Galatians 3:28

There's neither
      Jew or Greek,
there's neither
      slave or free
there's neither
      male or female
          It's by grace He sets you free
His children are one people
The bride of the great Son
So glorify the Father
celebrate what He has done!

God does not,
Like you more
Based on who
Your parents are
God does not,
Bring you in
Based on your
Financial situation
God does not,
Judge your merit
Based on your
Intelligence or talent
God does not,
Take you in
Cuz you try
To pay your debt of sin
          It's only by
          The work of Jesus
          And faith bestowed
          On whomever He pleases!!

It's **not** about your

☐ race

It's **not** about your

☐ rank

It's **not** about your

☐ gender

Or your money in the

☐ bank

It's **not** about your

☐ culture

Not about your

☐ place

It's all the about the

Savior

So let's all give Him

praise!

We do love you
We do love you
We do love you
Jesus
The God who does!

The Lord God is Giant*

The Lord God is
GIANT

In power self-
RELIANT

Glory in the
HIGHEST

Boundless love
DEFINED &

The Lord God is
GIANT

What burden can He not carry?
What fire can He not pass through?
What single thing
can He not work out for good?
What heart can He not renew?

What storm can He not contain?
What evil can He not restrain?
What single righteous judgment
can He not bestow?
Who can stop His "Let my people go!"

No king could defeat Him
No enemy destroy Him
No suffering deter Him
The tomb could not hold Him
No king could defeat Him
No enemy destroy Him
No suffering deter Him
The tomb could not hold Him

His love knows no bounds
The earth shall resound
His love knows no bounds
The earth shall resound

GIANT
The Lord God is

Saving Faith is Safe
John 2:23-25

Hear / Knowledge
Inside of, mankind is
An eternal soul that goes on forever
Inside of, mankind is
A corruption from holiness has severed
Inside of, mankind is
Easily deceived by his own heart
Inside of, mankind is,
Incapable of lighting the dark

God knows the heart of everyone
Do you have saving faith through Jesus Christ the Son?

Respond / Believe
Saving faith is safe
Saving faith is safe
You must know the truth of God
Of his holiness, his judgment and his love
You must know the need of man
That your accountable, enslaved by your own sin
You must know the gift of Christ
His sacrificial death and resurrected life
You must respond with true belief
Accept, lament, repent, rely and then receive
This is saving faith
Saving faith is safe.

Unsafe Faith

Now,
An Unsafe Faith, sprouts up on ground rocky
Uninformed, only believing while they see.
Untrue faith, cloaking sin or validation seeking
Unwilling. to submit to a new king.
True belief's more than just respect
or a one-time joyous moment

Unsafe faith is counterfeit

Remain / Perseverance

(Col 2:6-7;1:21-23)(James 2:14-17)
Inside of, new life is,
Walking and keeping in the faith
Inside of, new life is,
Not of works, it remains through grace
Inside of, new life is,
Rooting deeper as days go by
Inside of, new life is,
Becoming more and more like Christ

God knows the heart of everyone
Do you have saving faith through Jesus Christ the Son?

23

Mercy Waded In*

I am lying as a dead man,
At the bottom of the sea
In an ocean of my making
Filled with all my sinful deeds
In this sludge of my rebellion
Is my lifeless body found
Worthless, messed up and unholy
In this state I'm lifeless, bound

But then,
Love
came in,
And picked me up
But then,
Jesus
stepped in
And took my cup

And Mercy,
waded,
in
Into the,
depths of,
my sin
And gave this,
dead man
life
forgiveness,
in Jesus
Christ

In my works there's no redemption
And in nothing I can boast
In my body, there is movement
But in spirit, just a corpse
For my sins there is judgment
The debt for justice must be paid
That is why He went to Calvary
With His blood the payment made

But then,
He died
for sin
And paid the price
But then,
Christ
rose again
And gave me life

And Mercy,
waded,
in
Into the,
depths of,
my sin
And gave this,
dead man
life
forgiveness,
in Jesus
Christ

The Plan to Save the World
John 3:16-21

The plan to save the world
Through His only Son
Given though unearned
Wages paid; belief begun
That's the plan to save the world!

The plan,
It starts and ends with God
Fulfillment of His love
To save sinful mankind
In their state of rebellion

The world,
The people whom He loves
Both ransomed and undone
The transformed and the lost ones
He loves what he has fashioned

Two groups are all that we are in
The ones who are not condemned
And the ones condemned already

The plan to save the world
Through His only Son
Given though unearned
Wages paid; belief begun
That's the plan to save the world!

Receive,
Scriptures share his life
The signs' proof does suffice
The Father and I are one
Saving faith in the Son.

Results,
What the does the plan do?
Eternal life for you
And all who believe in Him
Are lovingly welcomed in

Two groups are all that we are in
The ones who trust in Him
And the ones the Son is judging

Live Like the Lord's Returning
1 Thes 5:6, 1 Cor 15:58, 2 Peter 3:11-14

-- 1 Thes 5:6 --

This is not the time to sleep…
Though others may be sleeping on the job
But it's time to stay awake…
Keep watch and labor til the work is done

We do not know the hour
We do not know when the day may come
But Jesus Christ, He will return
Because He promised us
So, Live… like the Lord's returning
Love… for the Lord's returning
Hope… in the Lord's returning, now

-- 1 Cor. 15:58 --

So, be steadfast and do not move
Always abounding in the work of the Lord
For your actions, done in Christ
Know and remember that they won't be ignored

We do not know the hour
We do not know when the day may come
But Jesus Christ, He will return
Because He promised us
So, Live… like the Lord's returning
Love… for the Lord's returning
Hope… in the Lord's returning, now

-- *2 Peter 3:11-14* --

Jesus is not slow in His return
But patient, not wishing that any should perish
His day comes unannounced. like a thief
So how should we live? With hope and in holiness
One day the heavens, will dissolve
All of what we know will be burnt away
The new heaven and earth will stand
In the Lord's power...What a glorious day!

We do not know the hour
We do not know when the day may come
But Jesus Christ, He will return
Because He promised us
So, Live... like the Lord's returning
Love... for the Lord's returning
Hope... in the Lord's returning, now

It's the blessed hope...
It's the lasting joy...
The glorious appearing
Of the Risen Son!

We do not know the hour
We do not know when the day may come
But Jesus Christ, He will return
Because He promised Peter & James, Andrew & John,
Thomas & Philip, Simon and Thaddeus, James & Mathias,
the other James & Paul, the whole of creation,
... AND ALL OF US!!

So, Live... like the Lord's returning
Love... for the Lord's returning
Hope... in the Lord's returning, now

A Letter to Gaius
3 John

Third John, a letter to Gaius from John

I, John, write to you Gaius who I care for in the truth
I pray that you will prosper
and good health will stay with you
I was very glad to hear
that you are walking in the truth
And I have
no greater joy
than when my children walk in truth
You have acted faithfully
to both the Gentiles and the Jews
Keeping helping those you can,
your fellow workers in the truth

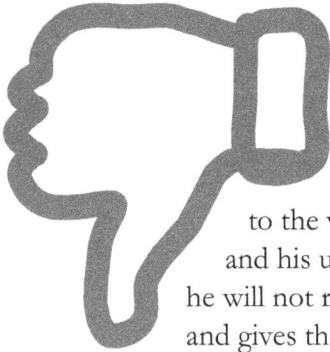

Now I wrote to the church
but Diotrephes did not listen
He likes to put himself first
And if I come,
I will call some attention
to the wicked deeds he has done
and his unjust vain accusations
he will not receive the brethren
and gives those that do excommunication

Do not do as Diotrephes,
do not imitate acts of evil
Do follow those who do good
act like those kind of people

For the one who does good is of God
the one who does good is of God.

Now Demetrius is a man
With a good testimony
Given from everyone
Include our testimony
And you know our word is truth
His life is backed by the truth

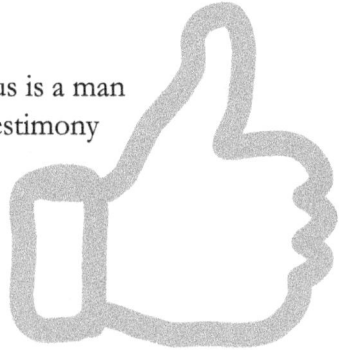

Do as Demetrius
do imitate righteousness
Do follow those who do good
Folks who are known as gracious

For the one who does good is of God the one who does good is of God.

I have many things to write to you
But I would rather not write them to you
with pen and ink

but I hope to see you shortly
and talk with you face to face
peace be to you
the friends greet you,
greet the friends by name!

OF
PSALMS & WORSHIP

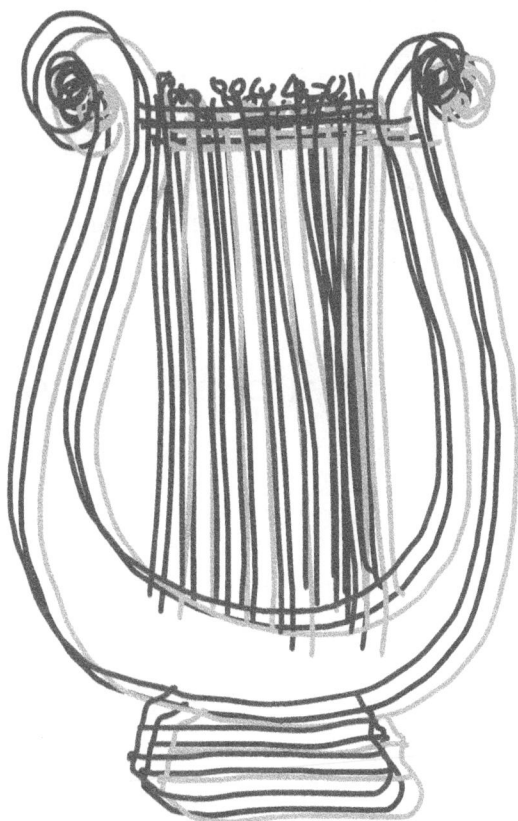

*I Love a Vineyard**
Isaiah 5:1-6:8

I love a vineyard, but it's gone wild
Vintage entangled by its natural side
Righteous grew to riot, justice run aground
I love vineyard, but it's time chop it down

Woe to the one who took, all the room, empty tombs
Forgot those in need, partied on, selfish deeds
Taunting God saying, "Let him come, bring it on!"
Choosing evil over what is right, dark for light
You expect rewards from your fields, but get the tissues out,
you'll be broken by the yield.

Do you remember when the field did shake, start to quake?
Your response to it was not to change, build again
Then your enemies' signal raised, they obeyed
The call to war to put you in your place, seize their prey
You expect rewards from your fields, but get the tissues out,
you'll be broken by the yield

I love a vineyard, but it's gone wild
Vintage entangled by its natural side
Righteous grew to riot,
justice run aground
I love vineyard,
but it's time to chop it down

Woe woe woe, sadly so.
Woe woe woe, judgment go.
Woe woe woe, lips on unclean
Woe woe woe, my eyes saw the King

I love a vineyard,
but it's gone wild
Vintage entangled by
its natural side
Righteous grew to riot,
justice run aground
I love vineyard,
but it's time to
chop it down.

Ascribe to the Lord*
Psalm 29

Ascribe, to the Lord
Shout it from the mountaintop
Ascribe, to the Lord
All the things that He has done
Ascribe to the Lord,
on the air and in your heart
Ascribe, to the Lord
All the things that He has done
All the things that He has done

The voice of the Lord,
Flashes with flames of fire
The voice of the Lord,
Shatters the strongest trees
The voice of the Lord,
Creates life out of darkness
The voice of the Lord,
Blesses His people with peace
Glory, Glory, Gloria!

Ascribe, to the Lord
Holiness, glory and strength
Ascribe, to the Lord
The glory that is due His name!
Ascribe to the Lord
Forevermore as King He reigns
Ascribe, to the Lord
The glory that is due His name!
The glory that is due His name!

The voice of the Lord,
is over the waters
The voice of the Lord,
thunders over the seas
The voice of the Lord,
shouts out with power
The voice of the Lord,
Is full of majesty
Is full of majesty

Ascribe, to the Lord
All the things that He has done!
Ascribe, to the Lord
The glory that is due His name!

Ascribe, to the Lord
All the things that He has done!
Ascribe, to the Lord
The glory that is due His name!
Ascribe to the Lord
All the things that He has done!
Ascribe, to the Lord
The glory that is due His name!
The glory that is due His name!

I Wanna Get Old
Psalm 71

I think, I wanna get old
Live, at least, another thirty years
I think, I wanna go gray
Stay alive, til my youth but disappears

Not because, I want a mortgage
no, no, no, no
Not because, I'll grunt when I stand up. and
Not because, I'll worry if those kids passing by,
will step upon my lawn

But so I, CAN, TELL, of you greatness, to the next generation!
But so I, CAN, TELL, of you greatness, to the next generation!
Your righteousness reaches the heavens.
Oh, oh, oh, oh
Oh the mighty things you've done
Please, let me stay, down here on earth-
Till I've told,
the kids,
of the Next generation

I think, I wanna get old
That when mocked, she-bears come to my aid
I think, I wanna live long
And have the strength, to clear the mountain that God gave

Not so I, can take it easy
no, no, no, no
Not so I'll, have hobby time for me. and
Not because, God owes me any ease in this life,
for anything I've done

But so I, CAN, TELL, of you greatness, to the next generation!
But so I, CAN, TELL, of you greatness, to the next generation!
Your righteousness reaches the heavens.
                              Oh, oh, oh, oh
Oh the mighty things you've done
Please, let me stay, down here on earth-
Till I've told,
the kids,
of the Next generation

You, maybe a youngling
You may be mid-life
You may be, preparing, to go off into that good night.
Regardless when you are
Or the years that have been
Prepare and share the Lord… with the next generation

So I, CAN, TELL, of your greatness, to the next generation!

So I, CAN, TELL, of YOUR GREATNESS, to the next generation!

Let the Earth Quake
Psalm 99

Let the earth quake!
Let the peoples shake and tremble!
Let them sing of your awesome name
The Lord reigns!

(v.4-5)
The King, in His might, loves justice
Oh Lord, you established equity
You, executed, justice and righteousness
Holy is He!

(v.6-7)
You count, Moses and Aaron
As priests, of your nation holy
In the pillar of cloud from the heavens
To Your people You did speak

(v.8)
Oh Lord You answered Your people
And their trespasses forgave
But avenged their sinful actions
Over, and yes over, again

(v.9)
Exalt, the Lord, our God
Worship in Spirit, worship Him in Spirit and in Truth
Exalt, the Lord, our God
Declare His holiness, declare His holiness a-new
Exalt, the Lord, our God
Worship in Spirit, worship Him in Spirit and in Truth
Exalt, the Lord, our God
Declare His holiness, declare His holiness a-new

Let the earth qvake
Let the peoples
Shake and tremble
Let them sing
of yovr awesome
name
The Lord reigns

A Cry for Discernment
Proverbs 2:1-15

Father,
we cry out,
to have understanding
Lord,
please let us,
discern paths of right
We seek her as silver,
as for hidden treasures
Our ears are listening

The Lord,
grants wisdom,
His mouth
understanding
His Word,
brings pleasant-
-ness to our hearts
Discretion will guard us,
knowledge attends us
The Lord, a shield to souls

You are, a store-house of wisdom for us
A Shield, as we walk with integrity
And we cry out, for discernment
Our need, for understanding

As we
Under-
-stand Your wisdom
Our hum-
 bled hearts
discern and will be
freed by your power
from enticements of darkness
To keep on paths of life

You are, a store-house of wisdom for us
A Shield, as we walk with integrity
And we cry out, for discernment
Our need, for understanding

You Must Be Born Again*
John 3:1-12; Ezekiel 37

I have studied, I have taught
I have seen what you have wrought
There is no one else who does what you can do
Oh, Great Teacher, I can see
As a learned Pharisee
By your works that God Himself must be with you

He answered
Truly, truly, it must be said
You must be born again
You can't enter God's kingdom
You must be born again

In a practical defense
Your way, it makes no sense
Our traditions say your obviously wrong
So, the Teacher clarified
Vindicate before their eyes
Of the water and the spirit, bones alive

He answered
Truly, truly, it must be said
You must be born again
You can't enter God's kingdom
You must be born again

It's not works or bloodline featured
None alone will understand
It's becoming a new creature
A total inability of man

He answered
Truly, truly, it must be said
You must be born again
You can't enter God's kingdom
You must be born again

From above,
From above,
From above,
Born from above.

From above,
From above,
From above.

How can these things be?
It's not fair, or right or free!
Please note the mercy of the serpent on the staff
And Nicodemus, you're the proof
Though so learned, rejecting truth
By the grace of God has always been the path

Truly, truly, it must be said
You must be born again
It's only through the Son of man
You must be born again

Truly, truly, it must be said
You must be born again
The only way to God's kingdom
You must be born again

There'll be a day
When Jesus reigns again on this old world
Like He did when this world was young
Walkin' the cool of the day,
with the first boy and girl.

There'll be a day
When the very King of Kings we'll see
And the captive heart will live life free
Of the ruin felt before
Unshackled from the former world

O Come, O Come Emmanuel
And reign in peace over us
O Come, O Come
Emmanuel
We'll see you,
as you are,

Glorious!

There'll be a day
When the family of God will be complete
From the corners of space and time received
Adopted all the same
Through the power of the gift

There'll be a day
When I'll journey out and visit you
We'll talk about all things new
it won't matter how far,
across that city where we live

O Come, O Come Emmanuel
And reign in peace over us
O Come, O Come
Emmanuel
We'll see you,
as you are,
Glorious!

We worship You as if that time were now
As if that time were now
We worship You in hope of glory found
In hope of glory found
We worship You as if that time were now
As if that time were now
Yes we worship You in hope of glory found
In hope of glory found

OF
PEOPLE &
PLACES

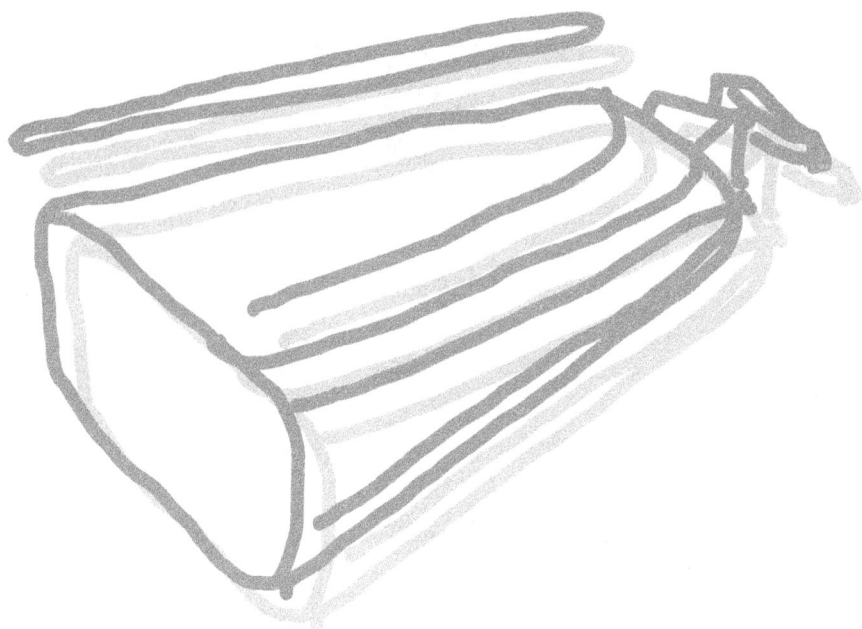

*Eutychus**
Acts 20

The Apostle Paul, in Acts chapter twenty
was preaching the Gospel in the city of Troas
It is a port town in modern day Turkey
Daily teaching and by then, seven days had past
He taught for a long time, for tomorrow he'd be leaving
The crowd in the upper room was listening by lamp light
Paul gave them the Word of God, they were gladly receiving
The talk went on and on, all the way 'til midnight
And that is when
all of the trouble began…

...Eutychus

Eutychus

fell out the
window

Eutychus

fell out
the
window

fell
out
the
win
dow

then... he rose again

Who was this Eutychus?
A young man in his upper teens
The sermon went so long
that he had up and fell asleep
No one extraordinary
as far as we can tell
We know nothing else of him, except that he fell
                    (from the 3rd floor, no!)
The first ones on the scene,
approached with dread
After inspecting him,
they pronounced him dead
Because...

Paul, seeing what had happened,
left the room and headed down
He came over to the place where
poor Eutychus had hit the ground
Paul grabbed the body of the boy,
and held it tight
He turned to the people and said,
Don't worry, he is alive!
        (brought back from the dead)
Paul,
the people,
and Eutychus
went upstairs and broke some bread
Paul taught them
'til daybreak
and the people were comforted
(the power of Jesus had been shown again)
                            When...

Melchizedek
Genesis 14:18-20, Psalm 110:4, Hebrews 5-7

Writing to the Jews
The author of the letter of Hebrews
Shows that the Law and the Prophets were good and true
But their fulfillment by Jesus was better... even better
It is a good thing to be part of the nation
That shows us God's love and His consecration
The traditions and leaders deserve our adoration
But those don't justify; don't neglect His great salvation

The Word shows that though...
Moses was there when God parted the sea
And Abraham was willing to sacrifice everything
That Jesus is greater than these and all the rest
And He does this by reminding them of... Melchizedek

Jesus is better than Abraham
who fathered the Jews but was subject to a man

Jesus is a priest but not of Abraham
the Levites through Abram gave tithes unto another man

Jesus is priest after Melchizedek
with no beginning or end, but a priest that serves forever

Jesus is King and Priest like Melchizedek

but the Son of God, which makes him

i n f i n i t e l y

better!

Melchizedek was the king
in the town known as Salem
before Israel was around
It would later be called the city of Jerusalem.
and when Abram,
before The Lord changed name to Abraham,
recued his nephew Lot
when the local kings had captured him while warrin'.

Now when Abram went to free Lot
he had taken three hundred and eighteen men to fight
and when they went,
he took the spoils of war which were his right
and while he returned,
Melchizedek went to meet him when he came into sight
and he blessed Abraham
for Melchizedek was also the priest of the Most High

If Abraham is the father
of those that were given the law
patriarch of the Jews.
He, first man of those that God did call
then both the tribe of Levi
and the tribe of Judah
paid homage to Melchizedek
through the actions of their Father

Since Jesus is the Great High Priest
after the order of Melchizedek as Hebrews five says
and it is beyond dispute,
by the created the lesser one is truly blessed
then the Levitical priesthood
cannot help sinners obtain forgiveness
but by His resurrection,

that Jesus guarantees a better covenant.

Felix (Ruler Trilogy One)
Acts 23 & 24

Now, the Roman soldiers of Felix the governor
had put Paul safely away in their barracks
for they were afraid he would die there that day
as the people there at the trial had become violent
For Paul cautioned these, he was a Pharisee
So the Pharisees said they could find no fault in him
But the Sadducees raged, rose against him that day
For they don't believe in spirits or resurrection

Then in the barracks
The Lord
appeared
to Paul and said
'Take courage, for as you have testified of me in Jerusalem,
you will also
testify of me in Rome.'

When the next morning rose, forty Jews took an oath
to eat or drink nothing until they had killed Paul
Told chief priests their plan, to have that traitor brought down
and on the road end his life once and for all.
Now Paul's sister's son had heard what they'd done
so he ran to the barracks to tell Paul of their plan
and the tribute as well, and so the tribute then said
'You told me about these things go and tell no man."

And the tribute,
named Claudias Lysias,
being in charge of the soldiers said
'Get two hundred soldiers,
with seventy horsemen and two hundred spearmen,
leave at nine pm
and get Paul safely to Felix!'
For...

Felix, knew about the Way
what they called back in Paul's day
a belief in Jesus Christ as Lord and Savior
In fact, his knowledge was accurate
Having a wife who was Jewish

But he also desired to do the priests a favor

When the soldiers arrived with Paul quite alive
they took him to stay in the palace of Herod.
Ananias, the high priest, some elders and an attorney
named Tertullus took five days, then Paul was summoned.

Then Tertullus the attorney spoke and said,
'Most excellent Felix
Since through you we have enjoyed much peace
and by your foresight you have made such a difference
our thankfulness will never cease
we won't waste your time, but hear us in your kindness
This Paul has been to us a plague
he causes riots among the Jews throughout the world
he's the leader of the Nazarene sect
He even tried to profane our sacred temple
By examining him yourself
You'll find out all things
are as
we
said.'

All the Jews there agreed, and confirmed these misdeeds
then Felix the governor nodded for Paul's turn
Paul began to speak, and said to authority
'I'm glad you're the judge since you know Jewish culture...'

'…Just twelve days ago, I went to the temple
to worship The Lord and there was no riot
I was not disputing in the synagogue or the city
they can not prove what they said; they can't deny it
But this I confess to you, the faith of the Way is true
Its almost the same though one major difference
We believe in God, the prophets and the law
and the resurrection of the just and unjust
But some Jews from Asia, who made this accusation
Who should be here but sent these men instead
Don't believe as these do and what we all hold true
I am here on trial for the resurrection of the dead'

So Felix waited for the tribune himself
to arrive
and testify of what had happened
before making a verdict.
He told the guards to treat Paul well,
then he
and his wife Drusilla
came down to talk to Paul themselves.

Paul told them about the Way
faith in Jesus is what saves
and about self-control and coming judgement
At this idea Felix was abhorred
He wanted grace without a Lord

And so he wanted to have no part of it

So he left Paul in prison,

talking to him occasionally,

hoping Paul would pay him money to be released.

And after two long years,

in order to do the Jews a favor,

he left Paul in prison

for his successor, Festus, to deal with.

Felix knew about the Way

But he also desired to do the priests a favor

And so he wanted to have no part of it.

Festus (Ruler Trilogy Two)
Acts 25

I
went up to Jerusalem
The chief priests bought a case against this man, Paul
They wanted me
to bring him back to them
to try him in a religious court of law
But, unbeknownst to me,
They had a more nefarious scheme
To kill him on the way back to Jerusalem
But Caesarea is where Paul was kept
and I would return there myself
So I told them to come bring their charges against him

These men,
who are here to accuse him,
I want to appease them
But their faith I do not understand
This man,
believes in a dead man
Has his religion
And says that the man named Jesus rose again

The only reason
I had to deal with any of this
was because Felix the former governor left it to me
So I stayed
in Jerusalem eight or ten days
The next day, after I got back, the court convened
Then we heard
All the charges now conferred
On this problem of a person they wanted hence
removed
but there were charges they couldn't prove
so the time had now come to let Paul speak in his own defense

These men,
who are here to accuse him
I want to appease them
But their faith I do not understand
This man
believes in a dead man
Has his religion
And says that the man named Jesus rose again

'Not against Jewish Law,
or God's temple or Caesar
have I committed even one single offense.'
So I asked Paul,
'Do you want to go back to Jerusalem
and let that be the place where a new trial would commence.'
My reason was easy to see
I wanted the Jews to be happy with me
but Paul said, 'Here in Caesar's court is where I should be tried
to the Jews I've done nothing wrong
but with your ruling I will go along
but I should not be given to them if their charges are lies'

He appealed to Caesar.
I, Festus conferred
with my counsel, 'Let the record show
before Caesar
Paul, you wish to be heard
And so, to Caesar now you shall go!'

King Agrippa (Ruler Trilogy Three)
Acts 26

I, King Agrippa, was invited by Festus
To come to Caesarea, with my wife Bernice
After a few days, he asked me about a case that was left to him
By the former governor, that went by the name Felix

Festus, told me, of this man named Paul
That the Jews who charged him,
the high priest and men of Jerusalem
and that Paul said for his defense, that he had done nothing wrong
And did not fear death, but for false charges,
he had appealed to Caesar

I wanted to hear this man,
so the next day my wife and I
arrived with great pomp and circumstance
Festus said before the assembly, that Paul was not worthy of death
So I bring him before you, dear King,
to see if any charges should be written of him

Now I have knowledge of the Jews
Their customs, ways, laws and beliefs
And that is why Paul told the crowd
that he was glad to stand before me
Paul, told us, in his defense, how he had lived, a Pharisee
For belief in the promise the Jews had long ago received
and to which the twelve tribes had hope to obtain
As they worshipped The Lord their God both night and day
Only for one reason am I on trial, Paul said
because I believe that God raises the dead

Paul then, told us, the details of his own conversion
And how that Jesus, now alive, had given him new purpose
To be a servant and witness of what he had seen
To both the Jews and the Gentiles, regardless of race or creed

To open their eyes to light from the darkness
From the power of Satan to God, and receive forgiveness
From sinfulness to sanctified, by faith in Jesus
The Holy One, Messiah, the Great Jehovah

Then Paul told me he did what God said
"I told those in Damascus and Jerusalem
Throughout Judea and then to the Gentiles
Telling them to repent and be reconciled
This is the reason why the Jews tried to kill me
And with God's protection, I am testifying
Of what the prophets and Moses said would come to pass
that the Christ must suffer first and then rise from the dead."

Festus stood and loudly proclaimed
That Paul had gone insane
That all his studyin'
was troublin'
and made him lose his brain
But Paul said in kind
I'm not out of my mind
my words are truth
Past the test of a rational mind
And I appeal to you
King Agrippa it's true
You've heard of Jesus yourself
You know the things he can do
I know you believe
What trusted prophets received
Works not done in a corner
Dear king do you believe?
Then I the King replied
Would you persuade me to be a Christian in a short time?
And Paul said, no matter how long it takes,
I pray that everyone here would might be as I,

except these chains!

I stood with my wife
and left the assembly with our friends
and told them this man Paul,
did not deserve to be put to death
or even in-prisoned,
but I will have to send him to Rome
He could have been set free,
if it were up to me,
but he has already appealed to Caesar

And so begins Paul's journey,
to Italy,
found in Acts 27 and 28
but did I,
King Agrippa,
believe in Jesus,
well,
the Bible doesn't tell of my fate.

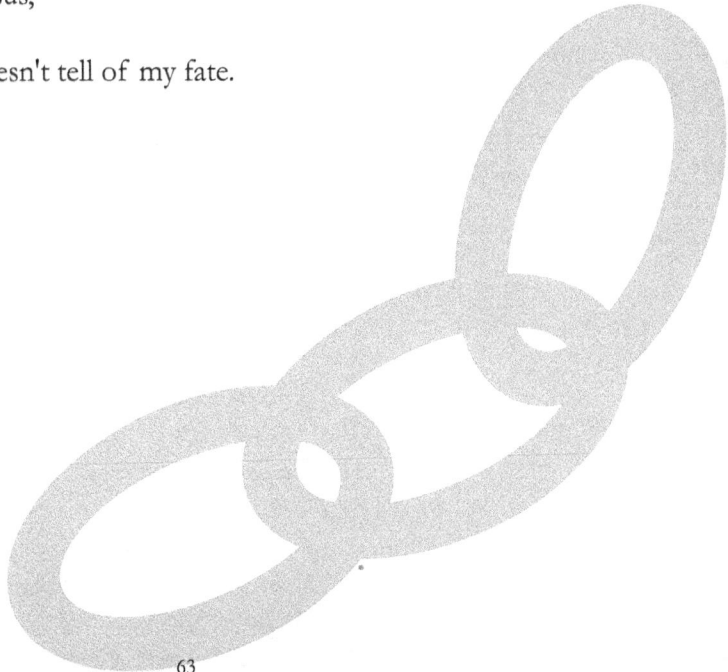

Sisera / Deborah*
Judges 4

My name is Sisera, I thought I was unstoppable
Til I met God's people, and then they did the impossible
My name is Deborah, I am the judge in Israel
I serve Jehovah God, and He said the armies of Canaan would fail

I serve the mighty king Jabin
I am the general of the massive armies of the land of Canaan
My forces are invisible
I have nine hundred iron chariots at my disposal
You have good reason to fear me,
I invade, I oppress and deal with conquered nations most severely
I will defeat you and not let you go
For example I captured the Hebrew people twenty years ago

I am a judge and a prophetess
The Lord gave me His Word in this time of unrest
His people had turned back to idols again
After The Lord had Ehud rise up and free this land
So to turn us back to Him
We reaped being sold into the hand of Jabin
The people waited twenty years to cry out to God
But when they did, God kept His promise, took His hand off the judgment rod

My name is Sisera, I thought I was unstoppable
Til I met God's people, and then they did the impossible

My name is Deborah, I am the judge in Israel
I serve Jehovah God, and He said the armies of Canaan would fail

I sent for Barak to come to me
God will win this battle and you will lead this army
March to Mount Tabor with a thousand men
Have them come from the tribes of Naphtali and Zebulon
Barak said, I will go with you But if you don't go into battle, then I will refuse
I will go, but honor will not go to a man
For The Lord will sell Sisera into a woman's hand

So, Barak is starting a rebellion
I will meet him in battle and watch his ragtag army run
With nine hundred chariots and all of my men
We will win this one because we win... again and again and again

My name is Sisera, I thought I was unstoppable
Til I met God's people, and then they did the impossible
My name is Deborah, I am the judge in Israel
I serve Jehovah God and He said the armies of Canaan would fail

I'm the leader of army that is unstoppable, unstoppable
But we were defeated by these Jehovah fearing people
Now my only concern is will I **survive**
I ran for my life, looked for a place to hide

Deborah and Barak, the judge and her man
We have to find Sisera and stop his future plans
His army's no more, his men are defeated
The battle's the Lord's, so let's go complete it!

I fled on foot to the house of Heber
He and King Jabin had a peace between them
His wife came to meet me and said "All is well"
'Come, stay inside' and her name was Jael
She brought me inside, she was so kind to me
I asked her for a drink and she gave me one so graciously
I told her stand guard, turn all seekers away
I went to lie down and she told me not to be afraid

But Jael was no friend to Sisera
When Barak drew near, she ran out to meet him
And told him Sisera was in her tent dead
For she had grabbed a hammer, drove a tent peg through his head

And God gave the victory to women that day
Between her feet, he bowed, he fell, he lay
Between her feet, he bowed and he stayed down
For while he slept Jael nailed his head to the ground

Nehemiah*
Nehemiah

Nehemiah, living in exile
with captured Jews, having been there a while
was cupbearer for King Artaxerxes
And on that day, for the first time looked displeased

So, the king asked, why are you so sad?
Nehemiah, for you're not feeling bad?
I'm not happy 'cuz my homeland's walls are down
So king,
if you don't mind,
can I go
 and rebuild Jerusalem

Sanballat and Tobiah
men of Haron and of Ammon,
who were glad Israel was beaten down
Sanballat and Tobiah
wanted the wall to stay crumbled and Nehemiah to get out of town

Nehemiah, when he finally got to town
Took a secret tour to see what was going down
But through the night, he found the gates and walls destroyed
He said rise up and build, but Sanballat was quite annoyed

Nehemiah told how God had sent him
with the king's blessing, to build the city up again
But Sanballat said 'you rebel against the king'
And Tobiah jeeringly said 'what are you doing?'

And Nehemiah said, We are going to build the wall
You have no claim here, God of heaven prospers us
The people rose up, and they set themselves to build
They worked, built the gates,
and in fifty-two days,
they had the wall rebuilt

Sanballat and Tobiah
laughed at all the Jews were building,
said if a fox jumped on it, it would fall down
Sanballat and Tobiah
plotted with Arabs and Ammon to come and fight Jerusalem

We won't let it fall. God is overall. This wall won't give in 'til God says it should end. We won't let it fall; we won't let it fall; we won't let it fall.

Nehemiah found out about their plot
So they prayed to God, and put out a guard
Their enemies said, we'll sneak up and take their lives
outside of town, the Jews said you should come and hide

But Nehemiah said we will firmly press on
half the men worked, while the others soldiered up
even the workers built only with one hand
sword in the other, for defense of this land

Now Sanballat, with his plot defeated,
Told Nehemiah to come out and meet with him
And when he didn't, he got an inside man
to try and trick Nehemiah to go to the temple,
but God revealed this deadly plan

So Sanballat and Tobiah
Rebeled against The Lord Jehovah
but couldn't stand against His wall
Nehemiah worked
to show God's power unto all
The Great God brought His people back
stopped the enemies
and showed Himself to be Lord of all

David's Mighty Men
1 & 2 Samuel

Do you know of David's mighty men?
Please allow me to call your attention
To how they fought for the Lord and to king David were sworn
even when he was despised by the nation.
and I respectfully apologize for any mispronunciations

Three Captains

The first three here are the leaders
the mightiest of all the men on this list.
They are the captains of David's personal guard
and had earned the positions they were in.

Josheb-bashebeth was the captain number one;

1 A Tachchemaninte the leader of all of them.
The mightiest of the mighty
and a spear wielder sublime.
He fought against eight hundred men

And killed them all at one time.

The second captain who fought for his king

2 and for Jehovah God his Lord
was the son of Dodo, son of Ahohi
the man named Eleazor.
He stood beside king David

when they defied the Philistines.
He didn't run away, he held his ground
when all the other Jews had fled the scene.
He struck down those Philistines
until his hand stuck to his sword.
A great victory was won that day
and of course it was brought by the hand of the Lord.

The third of the top three captains
3 was Shammah the Hararite.
The Philistines had gathered together
there at the place called Lehi
Where there was a fertile plot of ground
chocked full of lentils
All of the other Israelites had ran
but Shammah stayed and showed his mettle
He took his stand on that piece of land
against those Philistines.
He defended it from all his foes
and the Lord God worked a great victory!

Chief Leader

Now Abishai, the brother of Joab
and the son of Zer-u-iah
was subject to the top three captains
but leader of the rest of the fellas.
He used his spear against three hundred men
and dropped them to the ground.
Now of all the rest of the mighty men
he was the one with the most renown.
and do you know Ben-ai-ah?
Well, he was a doer of great deeds.
He struck down two ariels of Moab
and we don't even know what the word ariel means.
He defeated a lion down in a pit
on a day when the snow had fallen
and he struck, down an Egyptian man, with a spear in his hand
but snatched it out and used it against 'em.

An example...

Now let me give you an example of the faithfulness of these men.
One day when David wanted water they wanted to please him,
but David was just being longingly rhetorical
while evading the Philistines in the cave of Adullam.
Wishing he could be back in the little town of Bethlehem
and that is where the water from the well he wanted could be found.
Three of the mighty men broke through the enemy camp
grabbing water from that well and quickly brought it back
and gave it unto David showing their devotion to their king.
So, David, thankful, poured it out unto God as an offering.

More mighty men

Now the final group was the lesser
but still gallant, faithful and true
A fighting group was called a "thirty"
And in this group was thirty-two.
There was Asahel, brother of Joab
Elhanan of Bethlehem,
Shammah of Harod,
Elika of Harod,
Helez the Paltite,
Mebunnai the Hushathite
Ira of Tekoa,
Abiezer of Anathoth,
Ittai the son of Ribai of Gibeah of the tribe of Benjamin
And Azmaveth of Bahurim
Zalmon the Ahohite,
Abi-albon the Arbathite
Maharai of Netophah,
Heleb of Netophah,
Benaiah of Pirathon,
Igal the son of Nathan of Zobah

Hiddai of the brooks of Gaash,
Naharai the armor-bearer of Joab,
Eliahba the Shaalbonite,
Shammah the Hararite.
Ahiam the son of Sharar the Hararite,
Eliam of Gilo,
Hezro of Carmel,
Paarai the Arbite,
Bani the Gadite,
Zelek the Ammonite,
Ira the Ithrite,
Gareb the Ithrite,
Eliphelet of Maacah the son of Ahasbai,
And the one who was faithful though King David betrayed ya'
The Hittite husband of Bathsheba, the slain one, Uriah.

Now you know of David's mighty men
I am glad that I called your attention
to how they fought for the Lord and to King David were sworn
even when he was despised by the nation.
and I respectfully apologize for any mispronunciations

• • •

Big Faith

is the kind of faith
that trusts in the authority of Jesus Christ

Big Faith

is the kind of faith
that knows the character of the One on high

These ones, indeed
are those who believe
and have

Big Faith

A young Jewish man
who was taken from his land
told the king his dream
and then was seated at the throne's right hand.
The sorcerers agreed
being filled with jealousy
to devise a plan to end this man and renew their authority.
To their own God, they could not pray
but the young man did so anyway.
So, they threw him down there in the cave
but the Lord kept the lions' mouths at bay.
'Cuz he had…

A Centurion
living in Capernaum
came to Jesus Christ to see
if He would heal the legs of one
servant that he had
that was under his command
but he told Jesus to say the word
and healing would come to this man.
He understood authority
how the leader says what to do, you see
and the servant must then right now agree
to do what the master commands of thee.
'Cuz he had…

And time it does prevent me
from speakin' of…
…the one who offered up his son,
and the one who floated through the flood,
and the one who cried let my people go,
and the one who hung out the scarlet cord,
and the ones who won the victory,
and the ones who suffered great defeat,
and the ones imprisoned all alone,
and the ones they tortured, beat and stoned,
and the ones who gave their lives away
that this world has no right to claim!

This Tragic Freedom
Aaron's Song 1 – Exodus 7

After forty years my brother returned
Said he met God on the hillside
He had grown up an Egyptian royal
Not a slave, like us, for all our lives
Even as he ran away in fear
He thrived beyond our slavery
And now returns with a life well lived
Claims he'll set his former people free

Bondage has been the lot I've known
Our people groan for rescue
By the One that our fathers said
Had promised a land and life anew
As my brother planned for his return
The God of Jacob
spoke to me
That I would stand
at my brother's side
As prophet now
at eighty-three

Now the people saw us
as a curse
As Pharaoh took their
straw away
Their broken spirits'
could not see
Deliverance
was on the way

I cast my staff down before a king, and it became a serpent
Stretched it out over waters wide, and they turned gory fluid
Held it high over rivers deep, and a swarm of frogs released
Struck the dust and a cloud of gnats was found on every man and beast
And those were just the ones that used my staff
A decapod of tragedy
Now millions for millennia
Know that Yahweh is reality

74

Pharaoh's father had strategized
For his kingdom's power to remain
A generation's genocide
Would keep Abraham's people slaves
But he didn't know that our God
Had promised us we would be free
We didn't even need to fight
It was only Yahweh's victory

And I got to speak
on His behalf
And tell our people
of the truth
Lifting their spirits
up to see
That God has
Not forsaken
you
That God has
Not forsaken
you

And those were just the ones that used my staff

A decapod of tragedy

So millions for millennia

Know that Yahweh sets His people free

That God will set His people free

David v Goliath*
1 Samuel 17

I am Goliath,
I stand before your armies defiant
And you're not shrinking,
I am literally a giant
Why do you hide,
across the valley of Elah
If I were of Abraham,
I guess I would be terrified,
To see me, challenging you to agree,
To a one-on-one battle
for a nation-wide slavery
Your king Saul's hidin',
his armies are cryin'
You Egyptian runaways,
where's your God, I decry him

1..2..3..4..five, its go time, now you're battlin' me
I ain't afraid of no Fe-Fi-Fo-Philistine
You Bear-ly scare me, and I'm not Lion
I won't Paws when the vultures add you to their diet
How dare you try to stand against the people of Jehovah
He protects me and gave me the face of a cassanova
Go ahead and lift up your spear and your sword
You're already defeated, this battle's the Lord's

Hahahaha… Seriously,
my javelin's like the size of a log
This runt's like a stick,
do you think I'm a dog
That's easily beaten, your logic misleadin'
Send back Bo Beep,
his sheep need their feedin'
And when the next king
the prophet came to choose,
Your family left you out,
they've no confidence in you
You got guts kid,
but your resistance is futile.
The only fear I have
is that you'll break into a musical

Yes, you brought your oversized weapons out here on the field
But why do you need another guy to carry your shield
It's the armor-less poetic fights the iron-clad uncircumcised
a stone from my sling will be the last thing on your mind
The other stones for your 'brothers', heh, they'd flee in panic
And could be simply dispatched, by a lone, Jewish geriatric
A man after God's own heart states the Biblical prose
And now you'll have to play hmmm, shoulders, knees and toes

Keep up that confidence, your highness,
as long as you can
You'll need it, when Nathan says,
thou art the man!

I Lament
Book of Job

I wish that my birthday were purged from all time
I wish that my weary soul had never come to life
Let the darkness claim that day
Let the stars all fall away
And the sun upon my birth to never shine

I lament
Of the hardship that's now on me
I lament
Of the sadness that's within me
I lament
Of my joy that's taken by Thee
I lament, I lament, I lament

My friends sat around me
and tried to bring me comfort
And began to tell me of
the things that they now wondered
That there must be hidden sin
That I'd done to anger Him
To bring upon God's wrath in storm and thunder

I'm innocent
Of the charges they claim against me
I'm innocent
Of hidden sins within me
I'm innocent
Of a want of works done for Thee
I'm innocent, I'm innocent, I'm innocent

Then God within the whirlwind told me of what He's made
The smallest wren to leviathan, all beasts, mountains and plains
The Creator of it all
To the creature does not owe
An answer or does not have to explain

**CONSIDER WHO COMMANDS THE MORNING
CAUSES THE SUN TO RISE AT DAWN
CONSIDER WHO CRAFTS THE THUNDERBOLT
CAUSES IT TO SHOOT FROM THE STORM
CONSIDER WHO COMMANDS THE BEHEMOTH
AND WHO GIVES THE SKY ITS RADIANT HUE
WAS IT EVER YOU?
OH, JOB
WAS IT EVER YOU?**

I repent
Of the pride that welled up in me
I repent
Of questioning Your authority
I repent
Of my lack of trust now in Thee
I repent, I repent, I repent

I lament
Of the hardship that's now on me
I'm innocent
Of the sins they claim against me
I repent
Of my lack of trust now in Thee
I lament, I'm innocent, I now repent

Base of the
Exodus

I've
your mighty
How you brought us out
I walked across a sea floor
As you freed millions

I got to see you, with my own eyes.

mount

And in your presence, we survived.

Lord, thank you for using me,
Lord, thank you for using me,
Lord, thank you for using me,
Lord, thank you for using me,

And as I let my fear grip me,
I built the image of my own
I built the image of my own

Lord, thank you for using me, when I pretend
when I lead people away from you. Lord,
Lord, thank you for using me,

I had no idea up on the mountain, You declared your
To share your mercy and your grace. I had no idea
And my name would be the one you'd say,
For generations 'til the day,

Lord, thank you for using me, when I pretend I never met you.
Lord, thank you for using me, despite all that's happened. Lord,

80

seen
deliverance
of Pharaoh's iron grip
that was dry
with a pillar of fire

Got to eat with you on the

ainside

As you stayed your hand, we thrived!

when I pretend I never met you.
when I lead people away from you.
despite all that's happened
beyond the base of the mountain

You were gone; the people asked me
failure, acted like I'm not a golden tailor
failure, acted like I'm not a golden tailor

I never met you. Lord, thank you for using me,
thank you for using me, despite all that's happened.
beyond
the base of the mountain

sacrificial pattern. And my name would be the one you'd say
up on the mountain, You declared your sacrificial pattern
to share your mercy and your grace.
You'd give your Lamb, the Lord who saves.

Lord, thank you for using me, when I lead people away from you.
thank you for using me, beyond the base of the mountain

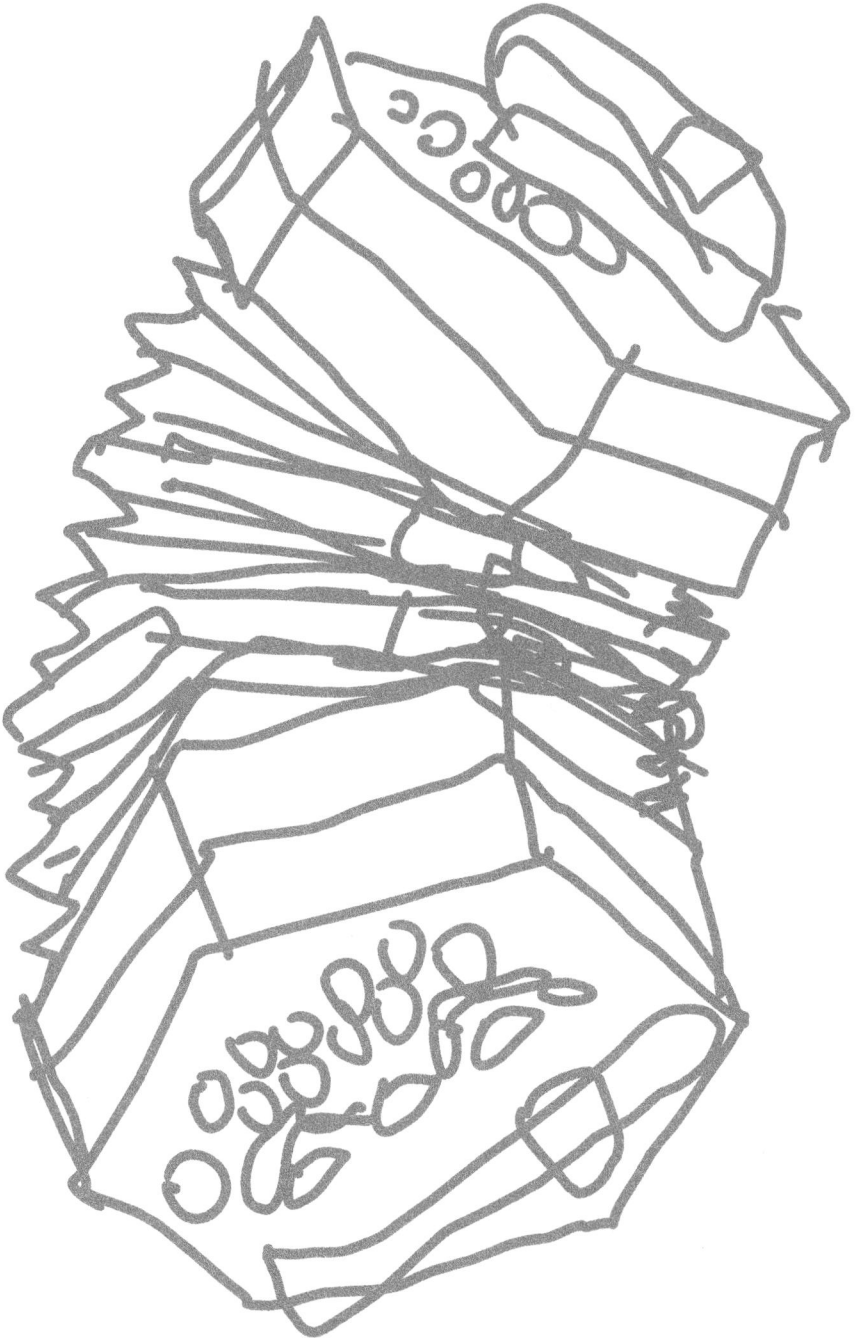

OF
STRUGGLES
& ISSUES

The Path to Contentment
Philippians 4:10-12

Contentment is learned,
it's not automatic
A state of being,
that takes some effort
On your part,
for you to remain
From both you and the Lord,
it works both ways
and He always sustains

Contentment requires,
proper perspective
Appraising Christ,
brings life into focus
In your strength,
you'll never succeed
I can only do all things,
Through him who strengthens me
In hunger or plenty

Appreciating Providence
The secret path to contentment
Appreciating Providence
Appraising Christ for all He is

Needs supplied, needs supplied
Wants are not required
Needs supplied, needs supplied
Not all our desires
Needs supplied, needs supplied
Wants are not required
Needs supplied, needs supplied
Not all our desires

Appreciating Providence
The secret path to contentment
Appreciating Providence
Appraising Christ for all He is

Absorbed

Sometimes I think I've got a handle
on my sinful self
Doing works, putting in the time
and helping others out
But those things I do can veil the truth
and from myself they hide
That a war still fights within me
and right now
the winner is my pride

I'm being
Self-Absorbed
And I want more
My life, right now, I live for me
Not thinkin' of eternity
Self-Absorbed
And I want more
These works I do I've done in vain
To hide the truth but their just wood and hay

The masquerade of humbleness,
in which I am
Shows itself when all the things
I've scripted don't go off as planned
And my words, in an instance,
prove the truth I try to hide
When they hurt the ones I love the most
who love me though they see my pride

Self-Absorbed
And I want more
My life, right now, I live for me
Not thinkin' of eternity
Self-Absorbed
And I want more
These works I do I've done in vain
To hide the truth but their just wood and hay

Search me, Oh God,
and know my heart
of this sin I do repent
Search me, Oh God,
And know my heart
lay down my pride, lift You up again

I wanna be
Christ-Absorbed
My heart is Yours
To this world it does not belong
But please remind me it is not my own
Christ-Absorbed
My heart is Yours
You paid for it on Calvary
Gave up your life to set me free
Please open my eyes and humble me
So I won't live so selfishly
I'm Yours

Search me, Oh God,
and know my heart
I am your slave for Your life You gave
Search me, Oh God,
And know my heart
You set me free so that I can be…

Christ-Absorbed

Floatin' *

I see others out in the ocean
I'm here, just floatin'

They seem to be ridin' the waves
I've been in this tide pool way too many days
I used to be out in the ocean
Now I don't swim, I'm just hopin'
That this flotsam at my arm will keep my head above harm
Cuz for now, I'm just coastin'

But the tide rolled in and left me here
I'm not trying to whine or be insincere
I just want you to know why I'm over here
I'm over here
I'm over here

I'm here floatin'
  - I used to ride the waves
I'm here floatin'
  - would surf out there for days
I'm here floatin'
  - I'm watchin' what I say
I'm just floatin
  - but the pressures got to me

88

My flood of tears troubles the ocean
I'm weary of my own moanin'
Each night I flood my bed with tears
My grief has captured me for way too many years
O Lord, please heal me I feel broken
Trouble down to my bones and
Be gracious to me, guide me back to the sea
In your steadfast love I'm trustin'

But the tide rolled in and left me here
I'm not trying to whine or be insincere
I just want you to know why I'm over here
I'm over here
I'm over here

I'm here, floatin'
- I used to ride the waves
I'm here, floatin'
- would surf out there for days
I'm here, floatin'
- I'm watchin' what I say
I'm just floatin'
- but the pressures got to me

Artificial Joy*

Artificial Joy
A cancer-causing packet filled with rue
Artificial Joy
The daily imitation of the holy fruit
Artificial Joy
Looks the part, but it's just painted on ya'
Artificial Joy
Known as toxic in more than California

I fake a smile,
it's just pretend
Enough to throw you off,
my broken scent again
A replica of who I am
Is what I'm wearing on,
the outside of my skin
If I removed this cheap façade
Would you behind your eyes
declare my lack of faith in God?

Lament and grief,
the psalmists wrote
They understood the need,
to shed their pious coats
Then why do we
think it is wise
And somehow sacred,
to wear a fool's disguise
The aftertaste, the cotter pin
That binds the falseness
to that malcontented saccharine

This world will
see His goodness
when His children trust Him
Through the good and through the pain
So if we never see
when we're suffering
who could believe a word we say
It makes you want to rue the day
That artificial became the way
To prove your love,
so show some dismay
and put your full life on display.

Artificial Joy
A cancer-causing packet filled with rue
Artificial Joy
The daily imitation of the holy fruit
Artificial Joy
Looks the part, but it's just painted on ya'
Artificial Joy
Known as toxic in more than California
in more than California
more than California!

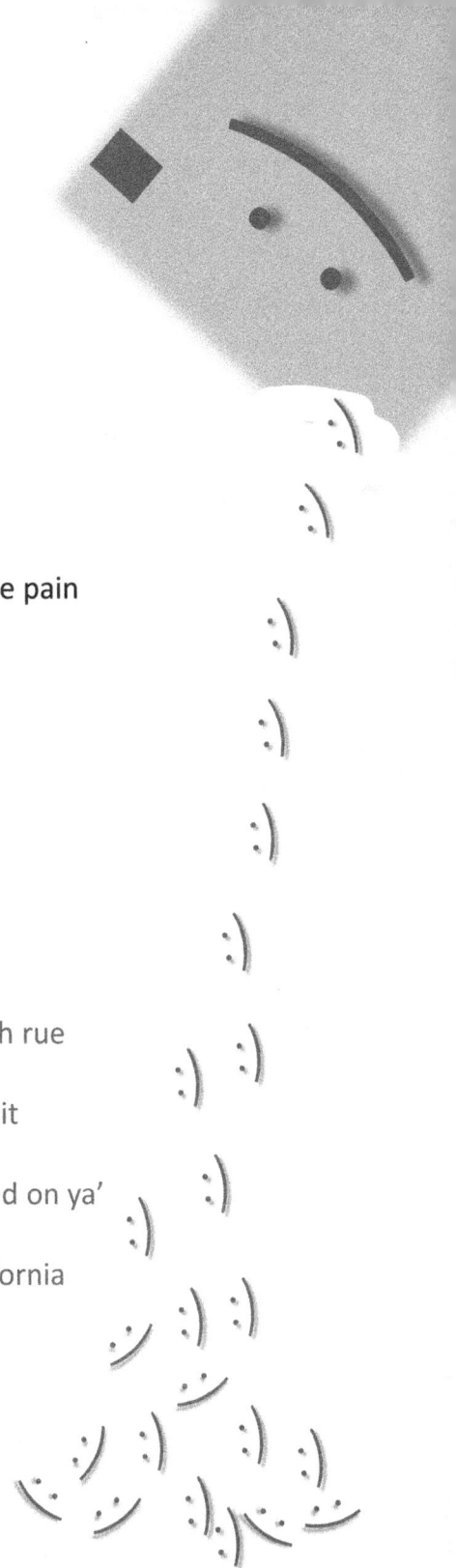

Take Care
Deuteronomy 8:11-20

Living in the suburbs
In the safety of the cul-de-sac
Where children play
'til the setting sun ends the day
And cars go out,
to and fro
With many places now to go
From practices and entertains
And grocery stores' options galore
There is a danger in the stands
That doesn't offer candy
or drive a paneled van

Take care
Lest you forget
the Lord your God
Take care
Lest you forget
who brought you to the place where you are
If you find you have some wealth
Or a semblance of ease
Work to remember that
The Lord provided these
Take care

Think about
what He has brought you through
The things you wanted
that He kept from you
The things you worked for
that He has brought to pass
But why you
when others haven't had the chance
Your power
your might
does nothing
But by the grace of God
it comes to something
And sometimes
it all comes to nothing
There is grace in those things
that come to nothing
Take care

Don't Empty Out the Cross
1 Corinthians 1:15-20

Don't declare to folks the Truth, with eloquent wisdom
Try, to design and craft a steadfast definition
Attempting to push God in a logic box forfeiting His
wonder
So you can ease our minds with a sense of human
knowledge comfort

The power of the cross is not
In putting all the pieces into place
The power of the cross is not
More meaningful if quantumly explained
The power of the cross is in
His personal boundless display of love
I Am, died for man
Revel in and be humbled in Wonder

Stop shaping the truth
to satisfy the modern Ancient Greeks
Enticed to nod their heads,
fulfilled in understanding more than these
Growing an appetite of next detail
instead of hands and feet
Thinking maturity
has moved beyond the
Foolish
bleats of
sheep

If we follow human logic all the way out to its end
Then God's best way to show His power's
to create the world again
A fresh world of peace
Sinless pasture for sheep
But He chose a way that baffles us, a world from sin broken
A place where most people do doubt in prideful rejection
He chose a different way
To die to give us grace

Please don't
TEMPT me
With the way you preach the Word
To try and tame the cosmic
in my hands
Please don't
TEMPT me
With the way
you teach
Scripture
^And *limit* faith
to what we
understand

^To don
a cape of knowledge
To trust
in human logic
To think
I've somehow got it

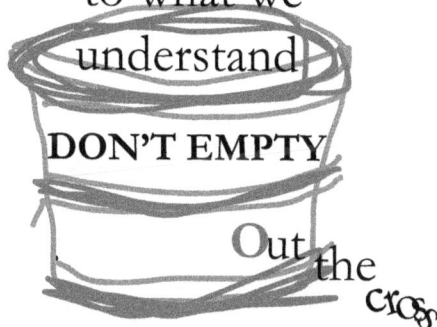

DON'T EMPTY

Out the
cross

I'm Distracted*

I'm distracted
And I think I've made it a habit
To find other things that I can do
To keep me from the mission that You put me to
I'm distracted
And I think I've made it a habit
To find other things to fill my time
Busyness is a spiritual pantomime

Binge Watching

I get done with my day and I wanna chill
Sit back, relax and take it all in
The evenings here, I got some time to kill
But the stories are good, and they entertain
I can't stop 'til the plot is all wrapped up
It's quiet in the house so I stay up late
Then the morning comes, it's hard to wake
No quiet time or I'll be late
Grumbling with no sign of praise
And my words all drip with a twinge of hate
To function at all, I need help you see
I'm on my third Grande coffee
It lasts long enough for me to get home
And then, please everyone leave me alone
It's been a hard day, can't you see
I'm feeling more than little grumpy
Then evening comes, some rest time for me
Now, let's see what's on TV
and it goes around again

Sports/Games

Whether right here on the couch or out on the field
I'm in the zone, on a team or alone
I'm a conqueror, all my foes must yield
And I feel the rush of the victory
An achievement claimed and I add to my fame
In what I set out to do, I can succeed
But the next day comes and the rush doesn't last
And I have a whole new set of tasks
They're not as fun, so I push on past
And the undone items pile up fast
And it takes work in this game to improve
I practice hard and I've paid my dues
So surrender your plans, and buy me new shoes
I'll be down in a bit, if I pause then I lose
And it is for amusement, by definition
I do what I'm good at and seek validation
Though in eternal pursuits I keep getting thinner
You can see on the scoreboard that "I am a winner"
and it goes around again

Social Media

I click on my friends and see how they've been
In just a sec', we can reconnect
If I'm the out loud one or introverted
I find out their needs and know how to pray
Post a verse when they hurt to bring comfort
And rejoice with them when they hurt to bring comfort
But the new reports they never end
And I saw my friend posted that again
I should say something, be a help to them
But I'll just complain and scroll on and then
Others seem to have no trials at all
They appear to have everything they want
And I contemplate all the things that I've have got
And my contentment melts in the wanting pot
And one of my posts got likes from friends
Oh I really needed that affirmation
See, that what I do to make a difference
So I jump back on my feed again
and it goes around again

Strugglin'

Oh, I've been strugglin'
Some may think I'm deconstructin'
But I'm not
I still trust, the Lord God
It's just been a hard time
Like cool walks, after the garden
And like fifty-eight of the Psalms

Oh, some are strugglin'
Friends may think they're deconstructin'
But they're not
They still trust, the Lord God
Don't help by omission
Or share God via definition
Maybe just sit with them in the dust

I can't sleep tonight again
The clock says four fifty-four AM
Sometimes it's my anxiety
That nocturnally robs me
Filling my mind with questions:
Like "Why did I let my identity
become so fused with my occupation
that when inevitably
change made its way
through my veins
I forgot how to be a person?"

I knew who I was
And I am still me
But it's takin' awhile
To be warmed again by Your glory
but You never went away

I've been walkin' in a haze
reflected moonbeam, out of phase
And at the outset
Those nearby would hold off judgment
When I answered their question:
Of "How are you today?"
I chose to answer with words honest
And for a while
They said they'd pray
But times changed
"True Faith should've gotten over it,
By now."

Oh, I've been strugglin'
Some may think I'm deconstructin'
But I'm not
I still trust, the Lord God
It's just been a hard time
Like cool walks, after the garden
And like fifty-eight of the Psalms

Oh, some are strugglin'
Friends may think they're deconstructin'
But they're not
They still trust, the Lord God
Don't help by omission
Or share God via definition
Maybe just sit with them in the dust

OF
CULTURE & COMPASSION

Never Meant to Be Gray

Never meant to be gray.
How to live, to love, to pray.
It's will never be OK.
To decide your own way.
How to interact with people.
Or respond to what they say.
Compassion tinted words of truth always
It's was never, never meant to be gray.

You may have heard it said, love your neighbors and your friends.
And to hate the ones you call your enemies
But that tone was not the plan, and you now misunderstand
How the love of the Father intercedes
If you only love those like you,
then "congrats you're like the world
And have forgotten that He loved you,
though no merit you have earned
Jesus took hatred and in return He showed to us His grace
"Take my tunic, take my coat, and also this side of my face"

And we know that Jesus threw those merchants' tables to the ground
Some act like that's all he did, ignoring all that's found
Two times he took that stand against those ripping off the poor
As they obeyed their Holy One, and travelled from all shores
So before your anger blisters 'cuz you'd do things differently
Your called to pray for those in charge and care for those in need
It isn't even backing down, it's living like above
'Cuz they'll never know you're Christian without love
They'll never know you're Christian without love
To care differently, the Son commanded us

If you brandish arms to prove your rights
and justify your side
Threat'ning foes with violence
in fisticuffs and type
And never listen close enough
to understand their side
Not to fade the truth
but to put aside your pride
No matter what those
so-called pundits scheme.
The end will never justify the mean.
The end will never justify the mean.

Together We Stand
Philippians 2:1-4

Souls unite, in Christ,
Together in full accord
Unified, same mind
All connected by our love of the Lord

Selfish ambition, put to the side
The gospel continues to suffocate pride
Reminding us that, it's only through Him
Our rebel hearts are saved from ruin

Let the gospel be the air that we breathe
An atmosphere of sympathy
Let the gospel be the air that we breathe
Affection abounds, joy is complete
Let the gospel be the air that we breathe
An atmosphere of sympathy
Let the gospel be the air that we breathe
Affection abounds, joy is complete

Together we stand
divided we fall
Bonded together
in the love of the Lord
Together we stand
divided we fall
Of one mind
in the love of the Lord
In the selfless
love of the Son
Look to the interests
of other ones
Together we stand

love
God

Teach
others

OF
OTHER
THOUGHTS

X

GARAMOND is the font for me
It's an old school book typography
Engraved with love by a man named Claude
That's a punch cut above other serif ones
Now That's a fancy font!

I like a Fancy Font
With serifs or sans, I'll take all that you've got
I like a fancy font
Ordinary words have an extra spark
With a Fancy Font!

TIMES NEW ROMAN set the pace
As the de facto standard print typeface
British conceived for the '31 Times
It lives, as default, in web design
Now that's a Fancy Font

I like a Fancy Font
With serifs or sans, I'll take all that you've got
I like a fancy font
Ordinary words have an extra spark
With a Fancy Font!

FUTURA dropped the serif for geometry
Featured in the titles of modern movies
Loved by Wes and Stanley, it's first in their hearts
But it must claim 2nd to forgotten Erbar
Now that's a Fancy Font!

I like a Fancy Font
With serifs or sans, I'll take all that you've got
I like a fancy font
Ordinary words have an extra spark
With a Fancy Font!

Now let's take a look at exceptions
Like PAPYRUS *or* COMIC SANS
Please never ever use them
Unless you're a HERO or Egyptian
And you still might regret your ♎ⅿ ♏✦✦□■
aka 'decision'

I like a Fancy Font
With serifs or sans, I'll take all that you've got
I like a fancy font
Ordinary words have an extra spark
With a Fancy Font!

I'm Writing a Book

Acting all drivin'
While consciously spinnin'
Maintaining a dignified look
No one can judge what is
Always unfinished
The key phrase to keep me off the hook
"I'm writin' a book"

"What irons do you have in the fire?"
"What direction are you plannin' to go?"
When you don't have a strong enough answer
There's an option that will lift you up above the status quo

When you're feeling rather listless
Lazy bobbin' to and fro
Instead of working to move on up ahead
You binge watch again your favorite show

Hoping you will be discovered
Thinking it won't take much work
And that the gifted never practice
But don't be fooled, time and effort the productive do not shirk

Completed project status: eighty-five percent
Almost done, no matter how much you've worked on them
Can't be judged for ill or for better
As truthful as those who predict the weather

Completed project status:
eighty-five percent
Almost done
no matter how much
you've worked on them
Can't be judged
for ill or for better
As truthful as
those who
predict the weather

Acting all drivin'
While consciously spinnin'
Maintaining a dignified look
No one can judge what is
Always unfinished
The key phrase to keep me off the hook
"I'm writin' a book"

Ghosts of Forts Long Built

Sifting though scraps left from other people's plans
Finding perfect boughs to bend to my commands
Carrying only what supplies I need
To satisfy my longing to live up in a tree

I can hear the call through those timeless woods
Beckoning me back to my careless youth
A melody on the wind, with notes of truth
I lean in to listen, listen to the...

Voices of the Ghosts of forts long built
Hearing voices of the ghosts of forts long built
Nostalgia's fog's waning, present joy not counterfeit
Voices of the ghosts echo clearly though the forts long built

That little boy in the woods searching for a space
Kept building more to set aside the loneliness he faced
Cobbled structures tryin' to make his mark
Distraction ends by sunset, then crying in the dark

Inside my soul, longs to go, as far as I can see
Into that past, free at last, no responsibility
But choice, brings with it purpose, growing in nobility
I need to be here and now,
I need to stay here and now,
I need to focus here and now,
I need to love right here and now,
Because God has put me here and now.

Voices of the Ghosts

of forts long built

Hearing voices of forts of the

ghosts of forts

long built

Nostalgia's fog,

waning, present joy

not counterfeit

Voices of the ghosts

echo clearly though

the forts long built

fin

just a little farther to go

I hope these
LYRICS
Have been helpful to you.
They have been to me at the very least.
Thank you for going on this
JOURNEY
with me.
It's nice to have company
along the way
isn't it?

If you find
YOURSELF
feeling on the
Outskirts of Venn,
don't fret.
There are
OTHERS
out here with you.
And the
LORD
dwells out there
out here
with us too.
where He made us to be.

You can find more of what I'm doing
if you are interested
at
dwaynesheridan.com

My wife & I host
House Shows
At our home in Oklahoma
for indie artists who we like
who tell tales of truth in song
we call it
Bard and Bow

I build props & costumes
mostly out of foam and such
I find it fun
and
it has bonuses like
we got to represent
The Wingfeather Saga
by Andrew Peterson
at the animated series premiere
in Nashville
You can see those costumes
and others
at
kadaloprops
on various socials

www.ingramcontent.com/pod-product-compliance
Lightning Source LLC
LaVergne TN
LVHW041229080426
835508LV00011B/1123